ON THE FIELD WITH . . .

ALBERT PUJOLS

MATT CHRISTOPHER®

The #1 Sports Series for Kids

ON THE FIELD WITH . . .

ALBERT PUJOLS

LB 1837

LITTLE, BROWN AND COMPANY
Books for Young Readers
New York Boston

Little, Brown Books for Young Readers

Hachette Book Group
237 Park Avenue, New York, NY 10017
Visit our Web site at www.lb-kids.com

www.mattchristopher.com

Little, Brown Books for Young Readers is a division of Hachette Book Group, Inc.
The Little, Brown name and logo are trademarks of Hachette Book Group, Inc.

First Edition: April 2009

Matt Christopher® is a registered trademark of
Matt Christopher Royalties, Inc.

Text written by Stephanie True Peters

Library of Congress Cataloging-in-Publication Data
Christopher, Matt.
Albert Pujols / Matt Christopher. —1st ed.
p. cm. — (On the field with . . .)
Includes bibliographical references and index.
ISBN 978-0-316-02701-4 (alk. paper)
1. Pujols, Albert, 1980—Juvenile literature. 2. Baseball players—Dominican Republic—Biography—Juvenile literature. I. Title.
GV865.P85C48 2009
796.357092--dc22
[B]

2008034006

10 9 8 7 6 5 4 3 2 1

CW

Printed in the United States of America

Contents

ON THE FIELD WITH . . .

ALBERT PUJOLS

★ PROLOGUE ★

Did He or Didn't He?

Most years, December is not an important month for Major League Baseball. The regular season is long over. The World Series has crowned its new champions. Spring training is weeks away.

But December 2007 was different. On Thursday the thirteenth, anyone remotely interested in baseball planned to be near a radio, television, or computer at two o'clock. That's when the findings of a two-year investigation of Major League Baseball were to be announced.

The investigation was aimed at discovering the truth behind rumors that certain professional players were using performance-enhancing drugs to improve their game. The use of such substances was banned by MLB; anyone discovered to be using them would undoubtedly find his reputation forever tarnished.

The investigation was ordered by MLB commissioner Bud Selig and conducted by former senator George Mitchell. Mitchell interviewed players, owners, trainers, and others suspected of using, distributing, or administering the drugs. Then he compiled his findings into a hefty 409-page document known as the Mitchell Report.

Long before the report was published, baseball followers had speculated that some players used the drugs. What they didn't know was who in particular was guilty. The Mitchell Report promised to give them the names of those players.

Throughout the morning of December 13, radio stations, television networks, and Internet sites buzzed with predictions of the names that would appear in the report. No one would know who was on the list for sure, however, until two o'clock.

Or would they?

A few hours before the report was to be made public, the television station WNBC in New York City and its Web site, msnbc.com, posted a list of players whose names supposedly appeared in the

Mitchell Report. The list was unconfirmed but that didn't stop some in the news media from reporting it as fact.

Sadly, many of those names didn't strike people as surprising. But for Missouri baseball fans, one name came as a shock: Albert Pujols, the 27-year-old first baseman for the St. Louis Cardinals.

Pujols had been a star slugger for the Cards ever since joining the team in 2001. He had the lean, muscular physique of someone who trained hard year-round. He worked long hours to improve his game; according to many, he spent as much time reviewing videotape of his swing as he did on perfecting its motion. He was also known for his strong religious convictions and his dedication to his family.

But was all that just a sham? Were his abilities really thanks to drugs, not hard work?

People wanting immediate answers to these and other questions would just have to wait. The official Mitchell Report and the truth about Albert Pujols wasn't due to come out until two o'clock. Until then, they were left wondering — and hoping that their loyalty to their favorite player would be rewarded in the end.

⭐ CHAPTER ONE ⭐

1980–1996

From Santo Domingo to Independence

Jose Alberto Pujols, later known simply as Albert, was born on January 16, 1980, in Santo Domingo, capital city of the Dominican Republic. His father, Bienvenido, was a well-known and respected pitcher for one of the Dominican's baseball teams. Bienvenido's job required him to crisscross the small island country playing ball, which meant he could not care for his son himself.

Baby Albert was in good hands, however. His grandmother, America, raised him along with Bienvenido's eleven brothers and sisters. These children were Albert's aunts and uncles, but because of their close upbringing, they were more like his own siblings.

Santo Domingo, like many large cities, had its share of poverty and crime. The Pujols weren't rich;

indeed, by some standards, they were quite poor. But they made do with what they had and rarely experienced want of anything essential. America also made sure Albert and the other children understood the difference between right and wrong. Her strong religious beliefs helped her raise them to be good, moral people who understood that taking to a life of crime was not a solution to one's problems.

As Albert grew, he did what many young boys in the Dominican Republic did. He went to school. He did chores. He roughhoused and played with his friends.

"I played video games when I was a little boy, but not that much," he once said in an interview. "I was more interested in being outside, and playing baseball. . . . I learned to play on the streets in the Dominican Republic when I was eight years old."

Albert wasn't the only young boy playing baseball. The Dominican Republic has a long and colorful baseball history. Researchers believe the game itself was first introduced to the island about a century and a half ago by people from Cuba, who themselves had learned it from Americans.

The game took root in the Republic almost immediately, thanks in large part to sugar plantation owners who encouraged their workers to play in the months after the harvest. They helped organize teams and create fields, paid for players to practice, and arranged games.

From the plantations, the sport spread throughout the country. By the end of the first decade of the 1900s, four official teams had been formed. That number grew with the sport's popularity, not only in the Dominican Republic but in surrounding Caribbean nations, too. The 1920s and 1930s saw fierce competition among teams from these different countries.

Players from the United States, including members of the Negro League such as Satchel Paige, also participated in competition in the Dominican Republic. They soon realized how talented many players from the tropical islands were. When they returned home, they brought stories and information about these players with them.

Major League Baseball didn't hurry to recruit Dominicans, however. In those days, professional baseball players came in only one color: white. In fact, it was an unspoken rule among team owners that no player of African, Hispanic, or Asian descent was to be allowed on to play in the major leagues.

That all changed in 1947, when Branch Rickey, president and general manager of the Brooklyn Dodgers, offered Jackie Robinson a spot on his team. Robinson's admittance to the major leagues opened the door for other players of color. One of those players was Ozzie Virgil, who in 1956 became the first Dominican to play professional baseball in the United States.

He was not the last. In the decades that followed, many talented ballplayers from the Dominican Republic had successful careers in the major leagues. There's pitcher Juan Marichal, who would later become the first Dominican elected into the Baseball Hall of Fame. Felipe, Jesus, and Matty Alou made history by becoming the first set of brothers to play together on the same team at the same time. And Manny Mota pinch-hit his way into the record books.

These players and others from the Dominican Republic were all in the game long before Albert

Pujols was born. But by the time he could pick up a baseball, he knew their names, knew what they had accomplished — and knew that someday, he'd like to follow in their footsteps, as other, more recent players from his country had done.

To get to the major leagues, however, he'd have to prove he had the talent. That meant practicing and playing the game as much as he could. Luckily, baseball is as much a part of the culture of the Dominican Republic as its language and customs. Finding fields to play on, kids to play with, and adults to learn from wasn't difficult. In fact, the only thing lacking at times was equipment.

That didn't stop Albert and his friends from playing, though. If they couldn't find a ball, they could use a lime. No bat? No problem — they'd swing a broom handle instead. And if players didn't want to catch bare-handed, they fashioned gloves out of cardboard milk cartons.

As Albert grew older, he spent a lot of time watching baseball as well as playing it. Sometimes he would go with Bienvenido to his games. Then Albert would add his voice to the cheers from the crowd while watching his father hurl the ball from the mound. During the MLB season, he would tune in to games broadcast on television. He followed the careers of athletes from the Dominican Republic who played in the major leagues, and dreamed of a time when he might have such a career himself.

That dream, it appeared, wasn't completely unrealistic. With each year that passed, his skills on the baseball diamond grew greater. By his early teens, he was one of the best players on whatever field he stepped on. When he was sixteen, his abilities got him noticed by some very important people.

Major League Baseball had long recognized that the Dominican Republic was a hotbed of baseball talent. Nearly every team had established some kind of permanent presence and recruitment system there. Scouts followed the six Dominican teams from October to January, scrutinizing players to see if they were strong enough to survive in the majors. They built baseball academies to train and educate prospects. They scoured the country to find and invite a select number of young hopefuls to the camps to demonstrate their talents.

In 1996, scouts for both the Florida Marlins and the Oakland Athletics invited Albert Pujols to take part in their baseball camps. Naturally, Albert attended — and like all the other boys there, he had high hopes for his chances of taking the first real step toward reaching his dream.

But to his great disappointment, he didn't impress either scout enough for them to offer him a minor-league deal. It would have been a huge turning point in his life if he had been able to prove that he had the skills they wanted.

As it happened, however, his life was about to take a turn in a completely different direction.

☆ CHAPTER TWO ☆

1996–1999

Adjusting to Independence

In the early 1990s, many members of the Pujols family moved from the Dominican Republic to the United States. In the summer of 1996, Albert and Bienvenido followed suit. They met up with America Pujols and others in New York City.

They didn't remain there for very long, however. For one thing, the Big Apple was an incredibly expensive place to live. And while their former home in the city of Santo Domingo had exposed them to crime and violence, what they had seen there was nothing compared to what they saw in New York City.

Albert himself witnessed something truly horrible one day. The sixteen-year-old was helping out his grandmother by picking up some groceries. Suddenly, he heard a loud bang. It was a gunshot! Someone a few feet away from him had been shot!

Frightened beyond belief, Albert didn't stick around to see who the victim was or who had done the shooting. When America Pujols heard what he had seen, she decided the family wouldn't stay in New York City any longer than they had to.

But where to go?

America was determined to choose a better place to settle this time around. If possible, their new home would have a Spanish-speaking population, strong moral values, and offer them the chance for a fresh start in their adopted country. She found what she was looking for in the heart of the Midwest, a small Missouri suburb of Kansas City called Independence.

Independence was already home to more than two thousand Dominican immigrants. A move there would surround the Pujols family with others from their own background. It would also surround them with people from all walks of life who shared their values and religious convictions.

When America learned about Independence, she decided that was the place to go. So Albert, Bienvenido, and several other members of the Pujols family made the move from New York to Missouri.

Anyone who has ever moved knows that it takes time to get used to a new home. The Pujols family settled in as best they could, and many found work. Still, there were plenty of challenges. The weather, for instance, was very different than what they had been used to in the Dominican Republic. On the tropical island, the early autumn months saw temperatures in the upper eighties and nineties. In Independence, those same months had temperatures nearer the sixties — and those numbers plummeted to the thirties and forties when winter hit. Such cold weather and the snow it brought was something none of them had experienced in their home country.

Of course, that problem was easily solved with a warm coat and gloves. Other challenges weren't so easy to overcome. The most difficult of all was the language barrier. The Pujolses had grown up speaking Spanish. Most had picked up enough English to get by. Albert, however, needed to learn to speak the language well. If he didn't, he wouldn't succeed at the challenge he alone of the Pujols clan faced: high school.

At sixteen years old, Albert was old enough to enroll as a junior at Fort Osage High. But because he couldn't speak English, he was placed in the sophomore class.

It wasn't that Albert didn't want to speak English. He did — very much. He simply hadn't had the chance to learn it yet. Then school started and he was assigned an English tutor named Portia Stanke. Stanke worked with Albert every school day. Thanks to her instruction and his own hard work, he began to make progress.

Still, speaking English during a tutoring session and speaking English in the real world were two very different things. Because of the language barrier, Albert struggled to fit in at his new school.

Then, two months into the new year, he tried out for the Fort Osage baseball team. He'd first asked the coach, David Fry, about the team back in the fall. Fry told him to come to the tryout session in February. When that tryout session rolled around, Albert came determined to make the team. He picked up a bat, took a few practice swings, and stepped into the batting cage. The pitching machine began to spit balls at him — and he began to send those balls sailing hard and fast into the distance.

"I remember the first time I saw him in high

school," former Fort Osage teammate Chris Francka later recalled. "The first pitch he saw in batting practice he jacked about 450 feet."

Fry had never seen any high school student perform like that before. Albert's swing was consistent and strong and his hitting was positively explosive. "He was a man among boys," he once said of the sophomore sensation.

Needless to say, Albert made the team. Fry put him at shortstop and then did his best to help the newcomer understand exactly what was expected of him. It often took Fry several tries and many gestures to get his instructions across to Albert. The language barrier was frustrating for both of them, but neither gave up. The coach recognized Albert's potential and wanted to help him improve. And Albert wanted to improve, for he still dreamed of playing in the major leagues. He knew that the better he did on his high school team, the better his chances were of one day realizing that dream.

✯ CHAPTER THREE ✯

1997–1998

Getting Noticed

The Fort Osage Indians began their 1997 baseball season soon after the tryouts. Almost from the start, Albert was a force to be reckoned with at the plate. Game after game he surprised pitchers with his offensive might. He piled up the hits and home runs, ending the season with 32 runs batted in (RBIs), 11 homers, and a batting average of .471. His talking bat helped power the Indians to the state championship.

Albert had proven that he could hit, and hit well. But he had also shown that he had a lot to learn as an infielder. Fry remembers that Albert often forgot to set his feet, the first step in an accurate throw. Often, he would then throw sidearm or underarm. Fry wasn't surprised to see such mistakes, because he was aware that other players who had grown up in the Dominican Republic threw that way, too.

If Albert had been a consistently strong fielder, perhaps Fry wouldn't have tried to change his motions. But Albert made several costly errors in the field that season. So Fry worked with Albert, teaching him a better way to get the ball where it needed to go.

Albert did the best he could, but he had been throwing a certain way since he was eight years old. Now, nine years later, his way had become automatic. It wasn't just his brain that had to learn the new fielding techniques; his muscles had to learn them, too.

Unfortunately, Fry's fielding lessons hadn't completely sunk in by the start of the 1998 baseball season. Albert was still shaky at shortstop — and to make matters worse, his hitting numbers were down. But that, at least, wasn't his fault. Coaches from opposing teams had seen enough of him the previous season to know they had to handle him carefully when he came to the plate. More often than not, they instructed their pitchers to walk him.

In fact, 55 of his 88 at bats ended in free trips to first base!

If nothing else, those walks showed two things. First, they showed how feared Albert was as a hitter. And second, they showed how patient he was, for no matter how much he might have wanted a hit, he knew to wait for a good pitch rather than swing at a bad pitch. And when he did get a good pitch, he made it count; 8 of his 33 remaining at bats were home runs, including one wallop that soared an estimated 450 feet.

By this time, several baseball scouts had heard about Albert Pujols. They started showing up at his games to see if what they'd heard was true. Most were surprised at the eighteen-year-old's powerful build. But these men were trained to look beyond size and strength, to analyze the player from as many different angles as possible. Some scouts were unimpressed by what they saw then: a mediocre shortstop who was walked every time he came up to the plate. Others were rewarded with displays of solid hitting, but couldn't get past his performance in the field.

"He was not the kind of player that was going to blow you away when you first saw him," one scout remembered. In the end, none of them was interested enough to open up contract talks.

Albert was bitterly disappointed but he didn't give up hope. The scouts had come looking once — all he had to do was get them to look again. And when they did, he had to knock their socks off.

He got his chance in the fall of 1998. It was his senior year in high school and he was playing with other high school students from around Kansas City in an All-Star game. One of the spectators at that game was Marty Kilgore, the baseball coach of Maple Woods Community College. Kilgore approached Albert after the game with one goal in mind: to recruit the powerhouse for his team.

Albert was ready to listen. He had already been advised by a few scouts to graduate from high school early and enroll in a junior college. Playing for a college team, they told him, was his best bet for getting noticed. If he stuck around high school for another season, he would face the same pitchers who had walked him his junior year — and scouts would continue to leave games underwhelmed by his performance. If he moved on to college-level play, however, he'd come up against a whole new crop of hurlers. Chances were, Albert would light up those pitchers like pinball machines. That was the sort of thing that got scouts excited!

When Kilgore sweetened the deal by offering Albert a baseball scholarship, Albert accepted. He graduated from Fort Osage High School at the end of 1998 and prepared to enter Maple Woods after the new year.

He didn't know it then, but that year would find him taking his first real step on the path that led to his dream. It would also find him meeting a person who would change his life forever.

★ CHAPTER FOUR ★

1999

Maple Woods

Albert Pujols was nearly 19 years old when he received his diploma from Fort Osage High School. He looked older, however, a fact that he used to his advantage one night. That evening, he talked his way into a 21-and-older salsa club. He wasn't interested in drinking alcohol, as other underage people might have been. He just wanted to join the throngs of dancers on the dance floor.

One of those dancers was a beautiful 21-year-old woman named Deirdre. The two met and danced together throughout the night. Afterward, Albert screwed up the courage to ask her on a date. She accepted.

Albert realized Deirdre probably thought he was at least 21 since he'd been in the club. He didn't see their age difference as a problem, but he thought she should know the truth. So, while they were on their date, he confessed his real age to her.

Deirdre took the confession in stride. Then she revealed two very important things about herself to him. First, she told him that she was a very religious person. She believed in following the teachings of Christ and in leading her life by His example.

The second thing Deirdre told Albert was that she had an infant daughter named Isabella. Isabella had been born with Down syndrome, a form of mental retardation, and would therefore face many challenges as she grew up.

Many men in their late teens would have turned away from Deirdre's religious convictions. Not Albert. He had been raised in a household with strong religious beliefs, so when Deirdre asked him to attend church with her, he went willingly. He soon discovered that going to church with Deirdre didn't feel strange. In fact, it felt very, very right.

As for Isabella, Albert felt nothing but overwhelming compassion for the tiny girl. "From the first moment they saw each other," Deirdre recalled, "Albert and Isabella have had a special connection."

Shortly after Albert and Deirdre started dating, Albert began college. He also began preparing for the upcoming baseball season with the Maple Woods Centaurs (now called the Monarchs).

Albert's confidence at the plate shone through immediately, before he'd even taken his first swing! That's because he chose a wood bat from the pile rather than a metal one.

The choice surprised those who didn't know Albert's ability to hit. That's because metal bats had been the favorite of younger players ever since their introduction to the game in the 1970s. Metal bats are hollow and have larger "sweet spots," making it easier to get hits with them. Balls hit off metal bats also tend to go faster than those hit off wood bats. According to many players, metal bats simply "feel" better, so when given the option to use one, they do.

Not Albert. With his wood bat in hand, he strode to the plate and proceeded to blast ball after ball farther than any other player taking swings that day. Teammate Landon Brandes, a good hitter and future minor-league player, was astonished at the distance the freshman was getting with the wood bat.

"Are you kidding me?" he said then. "This kid is right out of high school!"

Pujols's performance that first batting practice showed his coaches and teammates what he could do. During his first game, Pujols showed his opponents how powerful he was at the plate when he belted a grand-slam home run. He demonstrated that he could deliver spectacular heads-up plays in the field, too, when he turned in an unassisted triple play the same game.

Offensively, Albert was amazing all season long. He added 21 more home runs to that first grand-slam homer, plus 80 RBIs for an unbelievable year-end average of .461! He impressed on the base paths, too, for he seemed to know instinctively when to take off from one base to beat the throw to the next. Pitchers who feared his talking bat often tried to get him to back down by hitting him with a pitch. But Albert refused to be intimidated. Instead, he gave as good as he got, staring hard at the player on the mound as if to say, "I dare you to try *that* again."

Thanks to strong play by Pujols, Brandes, and others, the Centaurs reached the regional National Junior

College Athletic Association championships. They had high hopes of continuing on to the NJCAA World Series, but unfortunately, they ended their season one game shy. They'd have to look to next year to reach that goal.

What they didn't know was that they would go into that next season minus Albert Pujols.

⭐ CHAPTER FIVE ⭐

1999

Scouts and the Draft

Major League Baseball has an intricate scouting system for finding and assessing young players. At the lowest level are the volunteers who go to high school and college games to look for exciting prospects. These volunteer scouts report to area representatives who work for the major-league teams. If an area rep likes what he hears, he'll go see the prospect for himself. He'll then report his findings to a higher-level scout, called a cross-checker, who will pay a visit during a game. And so the information goes on up the ladder until at last, if a player is very lucky, his name will reach the top of the potential draft choice list.

A few lower-level scouts had been interested in Albert Pujols since high school. Mike Roberts, a cross-checker for the St. Louis Cardinals, remembered his initial impression of the budding slugger. "The first thing you noticed about him was his strength. . . . You could tell that he could hit."

Throughout the college season, other scouts echoed those observations. "I think this guy is going to hit for a lot of power," Jay Darnell, then scout for the Colorado Rockies, once predicted.

"What I saw in him was tremendous athletic ability," said former Tampa Bay Devil Rays scout Fernando Arango. "He just hit the ball with an impact that you didn't see every day. . . . The sound off the bat sounded like cannon shots."

But amid the enthusiasm for his offensive talent was concern about Albert's defensive abilities. Darnell wrote that Albert's throws were subpar. Others thought he looked out of shape. And many others raised a question that still dogs him today: was he really as young as he said he was, or had his birth records been fudged when he moved from the Dominican Republic, as had been the case with other ballplayers from that country?

One of the major-league teams decided that they would overlook these concerns if Albert could prove to them that he was as good a hitter as scouts were claiming he was. The Tampa Bay Devil Rays, like most squads, were always hoping to strengthen their offense. They invited Albert to come to a predraft tryout in Florida; if he showed them something special, it was possible they would select him on draft day.

It was Albert's first real shot at breaking into the majors. Unfortunately, things didn't go well. He faltered in batting practice, hitting just one ball as far as the warning track. To make matters worse, he was told to suit up in catcher's gear despite the fact that he played shortstop. Not surprisingly, his defensive play failed to impress.

"It wasn't very pretty," recalled the director of Tampa Bay's scouting program of Albert's attempt to play the unfamiliar position. That poor showing, plus his relatively weak output in the cage, led Jennings to conclude that Albert didn't have what it took to play in the majors.

Albert returned home disappointed but not defeated. He knew other teams were still watching him. Now he just had to wait and see which squad, if any, was interested enough to draft him on June 2.

Unlike draft days for the National Football League

and the National Basketball Association, which are played up for weeks in advance and surrounded by media hoopla, Major League Baseball's draft day is a quiet, almost secretive event. The selection process is limited to fifty rounds that add up to approximately fifteen hundred amateur players in all. Naturally, the hottest prospects are snatched up in the first few rounds and offered the greatest salaries and signing bonuses. Anyone waiting for a call hopes to receive it soon after the draft begins.

Albert didn't get one of those early calls. In fact, his phone didn't ring until the midst of the tenth round — and when it did, he wasn't even there to answer it!

The call came from Ernie Jacobs on behalf of the Boston Red Sox. Jacobs had scouted Pujols and reported that the 19-year-old looked strong. The Sox weren't quite as convinced, but they were willing to take him on if he accepted their offer quickly.

For some reason, however, Albert wasn't available to talk. Deirdre answered the phone instead. Jacobs asked her to relay their offer of $50,000. He told Deirdre he needed a reply right away; otherwise, the offer would be withdrawn.

An hour went by, then thirty minutes more. Finally, Deirdre called back saying she still hadn't located Albert. The Sox weren't willing to wait any longer. Albert's name — he went by Jose then — went back into the pool of draftees.

That's where it stayed until the middle of the thirteenth round, when the St. Louis Cardinals decided to make an offer. By this time, however, teams were not handing out big money to prospects. The offer the Cards made was for $10,000.

Albert was now faced with a difficult choice. Accept an offer he believed was far too low, but take the first big step toward his dream — or reject the offer and hope that a second, larger one would eventually be extended.

Even though he knew it was risky, he decided to turn down the Cardinals. But he did so for one very important reason. He believed in himself. He believed that he had the potential to be a great ballplayer and that he'd be selling himself short by accepting such a small amount of money. He was also hurt by the fact that he was chosen after 401 other players. "It did bother me, I won't lie, I was disappointed," he confessed years later.

Albert then decided that the best way to show the baseball world what they were missing was to keep playing. He joined the Hay Larks, a collegiate summer team in Hays, Kansas, coached by Frank Leo. Playing for the team meant Albert had to find a place to live in the western part of the state. Fortunately, Coach Leo and his wife, Barb, were happy to have him move in with them.

His living situation sorted out, Albert set out to dominate the summer league in the hopes that his play there would prove that he was worth a more generous offer from the Cardinals. And dominate he did! He destroyed nearly every pitcher who allowed him to hit, worked on his fielding and throwing, and demonstrated his instinct and knowledge of the game at every turn.

His hard work paid off. The Cardinals contacted him with a new and much improved offer: $60,000 plus payment of his college expenses. Albert accepted, making it official by signing the contract on August 17, 1999.

Albert Pujols was on his way to the big leagues at last!

★ CHAPTER SIX ★

1999–2000

Minor Leagues, Major Improvements

Albert Pujols started off his professional baseball career in the Instructional League in Jupiter, Florida, in September 1999. For the next few weeks, members of the Cardinals' front office got a good look at him — and an eye-opening experience it was, too!

Boom! Pujols's first at bat was a screaming line drive far beyond the left field wall. Mitchell Page, the team's minor-league hitting instructor, and Mike Jorgensen, the director of player development, sat up and took notice. The more they watched, the more they liked what they saw.

"How come he wasn't drafted until the thirteenth round?" Jorgensen wanted to know. He didn't really care what the answer was; he was just glad the other teams had overlooked the young man who was blasting them out of the park.

Pujols's power at the plate was obvious from the get-go, but his play in the field was still in question. He'd been switched to third base from the shortstop position he'd played throughout high school and college. His inexperience in this slot was plain.

When the Instructional League ended, Pujols returned to Minnesota where, on January 1, 2000, he married Deidre. A month later, he flew back to Florida to take part in spring training.

At that point, he knew he'd be assigned to a minor-league team. He just didn't know which one until he arrived. Then he learned that he was to play for the Peoria Chiefs of the Class A Midwest League.

Class A ball is one of the lowest rungs on the minor-league ladder. If Pujols was disappointed not to have been assigned to Double-A or higher, he didn't show it. Instead, he worked as hard as he could throughout spring training and then brought that same work ethic to the field when the regular minor-league season started in April.

He wasn't alone in his quest for improvement. The Chiefs manager, Tom Lawless, recognized Pujols's natural talent at the plate but also saw that the newcomer needed instruction on his infield play.

Lawless was a former major-league infielder himself. He took Pujols under his wing.

"He was a very good student," Lawless recalled later. "He worked hard and wanted to learn." With Lawless as his teacher, Pujols began to show improvement on defense.

Pujols also received some advice that helped his hitting become even stronger. When the season began in early April, he was an unknown to opposing pitchers. It didn't take long for them to find out about him, however. When they did, they started pitching to him much more carefully. By midseason, Albert realized he needed to expand his range. He sought help from Mitchell Page, the batting instructor who'd first seen him in the Instructional League months earlier.

Page was surprised. After all, Pujols was hitting .330 to .340 at that point. He'd been named to the all-star team, too, and had won the home run contest before that game.

None of that mattered to Albert. He wanted to get better. Under Page's tutelage, he did. He also put in plenty of time at the weight room, adding muscle to his frame in the hopes of adding inches and feet to his hits. "Lifting, lifting, lifting," he said of those days. "I worked hard to get stronger."

His improved performance did not go unnoticed. Mike Jorgensen began to pay closer attention. So did Dave Duncan, the Cardinals' pitching coach. A scout from San Diego liked what he saw so much that he put Pujols's name forward as a trade possibility.

In the end, however, Pujols stayed with the St. Louis franchise — but not with the Chiefs. After playing 109 games for Peoria and posting 17 home runs and 84 RBIs in 395 at-bats, Albert was sent to the Carolina League to play for the Cannons of Potomac, Virignia.

The Cannons were an A+ team. Albert would face much stiffer competition there than he had in Illinois. Yet he handled the transition with ease, impressing not only his new teammates and Virginia fans but the general manager of the Cardinals, Walt Jocketty, as well.

Jocketty was in the stands when Pujols came up to bat for his first game in a Cannons uniform.

Crack! After dropping behind in the count, Albert laced the fourth pitch for an RBI. He did the same thing again the next time he came up. Jocketty was delighted, calling the newcomer "an RBI machine."

Pujols added 8 more RBIs in the twenty games remaining in the regular season. He also had 2 home runs and a mere 8 strikeouts in more than 80 at bats.

The Virginia team didn't make it into the playoffs and Albert's season might have ended then if not for a strange twist of fate. In September 2000, several minor-league baseball players traveled to Sydney, Australia, to take part in the Summer Olympics. One of those players was Ernie Young of the Triple-A Memphis Redbirds. The Redbirds were the number-one team in the Pacific Coast League that year. When Young left for Sydney, the Redbirds lost one of their best right-handed hitters. They didn't want to enter the playoff season that way, so they searched the leagues for someone to replace Young. After looking at several free agents and other minor-league players, their eyes fell on Albert Pujols.

That Pujols was a strong right-handed hitter was unquestioned. But did he have enough experience to make the jump from A+ ball to Triple-A? Added to that would be the fact that he would be playing Young's position in left field. He had only recently made the switch from shortstop to third base — would be he able to handle yet another switch?

To find out, the team added him to their roster for the final few games of their regular season. After seeing him play, they felt confident that he could do the job.

This was Pujols's big chance, and he didn't let it go to waste. He played in eleven games in the postseason. His superior batting helped Memphis emerge victorious over the Albuquerque Dukes in the semifinals, three games to two.

Next up were the finals. The Redbirds were playing the Buzz from Salt Lake City. By the third game, Memphis was up in the series 2–1. Another win would clinch their spot in the Triple-A World Series.

But the Buzz did not fall easily. The two teams battled back and forth throughout the early innings; by the ninth, they were locked at three runs apiece.

That's the way the score stayed through the tenth inning — and the eleventh and twelfth! Then, in the thirteenth inning, Albert Pujols came up to bat.

Boom! With a mighty swing, Pujols sent the ball soaring for a home run! With that blast, the Redbirds took the pennant and headed to the World Series.

Unfortunately, the team wasn't as successful when they took to the field against the Indianapolis Indians in Las Vegas. The Indians took the championship in four games.

The Redbirds' season was over, but Albert Pujols was still making minor-league headlines. First, he was named the Most Valuable Player of the playoffs. Then he stood out as the top third-base prospect while playing fall ball in Scottsdale, Arizona. When that league wound up its season, there was just one question about the future of Albert Pujols: where would he go next?

His rise through baseball's farm system had been steady and sure. From his start in low-level Class A in Peoria, he moved to high-level Class A in Virginia to Triple-A in Memphis. While there were those who thought he should take a step back and begin the next season in Double-A, it seemed more than likely that he would be placed on the Cardinals' Triple-A team. The idea that he might jump right to the majors was rarely, if ever, discussed.

At least, not until spring training began the following February.

☆ CHAPTER SEVEN ☆

2001

Rookie

Albert had spent the little time off from baseball he had after the Arizona Fall League working out in gyms and earning money as a waiter. The salary of a minor-league baseball player simply wasn't enough to support himself, Deidre, and their daughter Isabella.

On January 16, 2001, he turned 21. A few weeks later, he reported to Florida for the Cardinals spring training. When he arrived, he was given a jersey with the number 68 on it. That high number suggested that the Cardinals' management had decided to assign him to Triple-A ball; the lower numbers were typically given to major-league players. Apparently, the Cards had figured they didn't need another third baseman because they already had two solid players for that spot.

They would soon rethink their original decision.

Dave Duncan, the Cardinals' pitching coach, had first heard about Albert from his son, Chris, when the two played together in Peoria. Tony La Russa, the Cardinals' manager, had had good reports about Pujols but hadn't really had the chance to see him perform. Walt Jocketty remembered him from the previous season's game in Virginia. When they saw him play in spring training, against veteran major-league players, they began to pay very close attention.

Offensively? He had the power, the mechanics, and the determination to send the ball into the stratosphere. Defensively? He had improved greatly in the past year, and now fielded balls with grace and threw on target. Attitude? He was confident without being cocky; his eagerness to play and willingness to learn shone through.

Now all that remained was to see if the skills he showed during practice were still there during game situations.

That spring training, two key Cardinal players, Mark McGwire and Bobby Bonilla, were sidelined with injuries. La Russa filled their spots with different players, including Pujols. He also put Pujols in positions he'd never played before — outfield and first base.

La Russa tested Pujols over and over. And time and again, Pujols passed with flying colors. "It was impossible to get him to perform poorly," La Russa later admitted.

By the end of spring training, Albert Pujols had earned a spot on the St. Louis Cardinals' roster. Now it was up to him to keep it — and that was something Pujols fully intended to do. He had dreamed his whole life of reaching this goal. He would live that dream, no matter what!

The Cardinals began their 2001 season on April 2 with an away game against the Colorado Rockies. Standing in left field, wearing number 5, was Albert! Less than one year after his first game with Peoria, he was in the starting lineup of a major-league team!

Unfortunately, the Cardinals didn't win that day, gaining only 5 hits in the 8–0 loss. One of those hits came off the bat of number 5 — Albert Pujols's first major-league hit. It would be the only hit he would get in that three-game series, all Cardinal losses, against the Rockies.

But the season was only beginning. The Cardinals and Albert Pujols were just getting warmed up.

St. Louis traveled to Arizona to face the Diamondbacks next. Pujols made up for lost time during their first meeting. Batting fifth in the lineup, he came to the plate in the top of the second inning. He liked the first pitch Armando Reynoso hurled and connected for a single into left field.

He liked one of the pitches Reynoso sent him in the fourth inning even better. This one he laced high and away into left field for a home run that scored Ray Lankford and put the Cards up 2–0. It was his first major-league home run and his first RBI, and he wasn't done yet. He got up to bat again in the next inning and proceeded to wallop an RBI double.

Three at bats, three hits, a two-run homer, and an RBI double! His talking bat had fans gawking and teammates cheering.

Pujols didn't get another hit that game but it didn't matter. St. Louis won 12–9.

The Cardinals won the next game, too, and Pujols collected another hit, a two-run RBI double. He repeated that feat again the following afternoon, against pitching great Randy Johnson. A photo of that blast landed in the pages of *Sports Illustrated* that week — and earned him high praise from his teammates.

"We all went, 'Uh-oh. We've got something here,'" said fellow slugger Mark McGwire.

Pujols turned in a solid performance in right field, too, catching flyballs and fielding grounders like a player who'd been in the pros for much longer than a year.

The Cardinals returned to St. Louis with a record of three wins, three losses. Their home season opener was on April 9 against the Rockies. They hoped to hand Colorado three losses.

Albert just wanted to play well before the home crowd. They hadn't had a chance to see what he could do yet — he hoped to send them home with something worth talking about.

He did. He came to the plate in the bottom of the second inning. Bobby Bonilla had flied out; Ray Lankford stood on first with a single. Pujols readied himself and faced pitcher Denny Neagle.

Neagle reared back and threw. Pujols let the ball go by for a called strike. He let the next one go by for a ball. The third pitch didn't look good to him, either, but the umpire thought otherwise and called it a strike. He was now down in the count, 1–2, so he swung on the fourth pitch.

Clip! The ball made a sharp sound when it connected with the bat. But instead of soaring true, it went foul.

Neagle caught the throw back and leaned in for the signal. Then he straightened and checked Lankford. Finally, he went into his windup and threw the pitch.

Pujols waited patiently through it all. He knew the pitch would come. And when it did —

BOOM! This time, the sound that came from the bat left no one in any doubt. That ball was gone! Home run!

Lankford rounded the bases with Pujols, grinning from ear-to-ear, coming up behind. It was the first time that a St. Louis franchise rookie had hit a home run in the home season opener since 1954!

That wasn't the only feat that got him the books that month. He ended the month with a total of 8 home runs, tying the major-league rookie record set by Kent Hrbek and Carlos Delgado. Those 8 homers were the most of any Cardinal that month; 2 of them had been earned on a win on April 22 when Pujols made or drove in all 3 runs. He also led the team in RBIs, games played, and runs for the month.

Not bad for a 21-year-old who had almost been passed over in the draft two years earlier.

But was April's performance just a fluke, brought on by the adrenaline-rush excitement of playing in the majors? And if it was, would Pujols flame out in the months to come?

It didn't seem like he would. Despite a hitting slump in early July, by the all-star break (a game for which he was selected as a reserve), he had chalked up 21 homers to tie the team's season record — and there were still weeks to go in the season! In fact, he was the top-ranked rookie in homers and RBIs as well as on-base percentage and hitting by that point.

His defensive play was just as promising — and varied. He played right field, left field, first base, third base, and designated hitter. Yet whatever was thrown at him, he handled.

"Right now, I'm just getting a chance to play every position so I just try to do the best I can," he said.

Doing his best also meant learning as much about the finer points of the game as he possibly could. Teammates recalled being quizzed by him in the dugout; coaches knew that when Pujols asked for help, he would listen and follow their advice to the letter.

"He's a student of the game," hitting coach Mitchell Page once told a reporter. "His maturity is beyond twenty-one years."

Tony La Russa agreed with Page about Pujols's maturity. "You don't do what we've done with Albert every day," he said, referring to the many positions he'd had Pujols play. "It is very rare that a player so young and lacking in seasoning and experience will survive. It has to be a special talent, not just physically but mentally, and Pujols certainly is a special talent."

That special talent continued to shine throughout the final months of the regular season. In fact, Pujols played so well that he broke decades-old records in several categories.

On September 19, just eight days after the terrorist attacks of 9/11, Albert topped a 71-year-old rookie record by blasting in his 120th RBI during a 3-RBI game against the Milwaukee Brewers. Two days later, he broke a second rookie record, this one for extra-base hits — and he did it in the most spectacular fashion.

The game was against the Pittsburgh Pirates. Pujols came up to bat in the top of the first inning and hit an RBI double to left center field. Then, for the next several innings, his bat was uncharacteristically silent. His teammates stayed on top of the situation, however, and going into the top of the ninth, the game was tied 5–5.

It was the Cardinals' turn at bat. Miguel Cairo stepped to the plate. Omar Olivares was on the mound for the Pirates. Cairo worked the count to 3–2 and then laced the sixth pitch to center field for a single.

Runner on first, no outs.

Craig Paquette was up next. He laid down a sacrifice bunt. Cairo reached second but Paquette was out at first.

Placido Polanco followed Paquette. He belted a single to short right field. Cairo raced to third. Safe! One out, runners at first and third.

Olivares walked the next batter, J. D. Drew, to load the bases. No doubt the Pirates were hoping for a double play to end the dangerous situation. It might have worked, too, except for the fact that Albert Pujols was standing in the batter's box.

Pujols watched Olivares's first pitch go by. Ball one. He tipped the second pitch foul. One-and-one. Then came the third pitch.

Pujols swung. *Boom!* He didn't just hit the ball, he crushed it! It soared high into left field and was gone, gone, gone! That mighty grand-slam home run, the first of Pujols's career, won the game for the Cardinals — and put Pujols's name in the record books as the rookie with the greatest number of extra-base hits, knocking off the previous record of 82 set by Johnny Frederick in 1929.

The regular season ended a few weeks later. The Cardinals, thanks in large part of Pujols's performance, had tied the Houston Astros for first place. The Astros were declared the division champs, however, because they had bested the Cards in the season series. Still, St. Louis had earned a berth in the playoffs.

Pujols was thrilled to have been a part of getting his team into the postseason. A glance at his year-end numbers showed just how big a part he'd played.

He led the Cardinals in batting average with .329,

in home runs with 37, and RBIs with 130. Those three figures made up baseball's Triple Crown; by leading in all three, Pujols was the first Cardinal rookie to win that crown since the great Rogers Hornsby in 1916.

And the accomplishments didn't stop there. He was the first rookie in National League history to hit benchmarks in four categories: 30 or more homers, 100 or more RBIs, 100 or more runs scored, and a .300 or better batting average. Incredibly, in all of MLB history, those numbers had been reached by only three other rookies — Hal Trotsky in 1934, Ted Williams in 1939, and Walt Dropo in 1950. Stan Musial, one of the greatest Cardinals in the team's history, had posted similiar numbers in 1952, but not as a rookie.

No rookie in the National League had ever had more RBIs, extra base hits, or total bases. No Cardinal rookie had ever had more doubles, RBIs, homers, extra base hits, runs, or total bases. And with 52 starts at third base, 37 at right field, 33 at left field, and 31 at first base, Albert may very well be the only player in MLB history to have started in four different positions in thirty or more regular season games.

Not surprisingly, Pujols was unanimously voted the National League's Rookie of the Year. He also earned his first Silver Slugger award and came in fourth in the National League Most Valuable Player rankings.

Pujols must have been delighted to have performed so well. But as rewarding as the records and accolades were, they weren't what he was after. "I am trying to get my baseball team into . . . the World Series," he said then. "That is the only record I want."

Unfortunately, that was one of the only achievements to elude Pujols that season. The Cardinals fell to the Arizona Diamondbacks, three games to two, in the National League Division Series. Pujols himself struggled during the five-game series, coming to bat 18 times but posting only two hits, one a home run, for a dismal .111 average.

Such a disappointing conclusion couldn't detract from what Pujols had accomplished in his rookie season. Yet when he hung up his uniform for the final time in 2001, he wasn't looking back on past glories. He was looking ahead to the next year and the challenges that awaited him.

☆ CHAPTER EIGHT ☆

2002

Stepping Up

Albert Pujols had been the big baseball story of 2001 — an unknown, 13th-round draft pick who just barely made the roster but wound up shattering offensive records across the boards. But in 2002, Pujols would no longer have the element of surprise on his side. Pitchers who had never heard of him at the start of 2001 now knew he was a force to be reckoned with, and they studied his hitting style carefully in the hopes of tripping him up in 2002.

Only time would tell how well they had done their homework.

Pujols had been busy in the off-season himself. He worked out at the gym every day. He logged many hours in the batting cage practicing his swing and then more time in front of television screens analyzing videotape of that swing.

He also made sure other parts of his life received as much attention as baseball. He and Deirdre celebrated their second wedding aniversary and spent as much time as possible with Isabella and A.J., a son who had been born the year before. Together, they attended church and generally enjoying being a family. In January, Albert had the pleasure of learning that Maple Woods Community College had chosen to honor him by retiring the number he'd worn his one year there.

When February rolled around, Albert set off for Florida for the Cardinals' spring training camp. He showed up in tip-top condition, ready, willing, and more than eager to do whatever it took to repeat or better his rookie-year performance.

"I just want to get ready to help the team out," he said.

Help them out he did indeed, starting with the season opener on April 1. The game was played in St. Louis against the Colorado Rockies. The year before, the Rockies had swept the Cardinals in their first series. Then, neither team had much inkling of what Albert Pujols was capable of. This year, they both went into the game waiting to see what he would deliver.

At first, it didn't seem like he was going to do much. Batting cleanup, he ended the bottom of the first inning with a ground out. His next at bat, he flied out to center field.

Pujols's teammates were faring a little bit better than he was at the plate. Going into the bottom of the fourth inning, St. Louis had scored two runs. Colorado wasn't far behind, however, having posted their first run in the top of the inning.

The Cardinals were hoping to break their one-run lead wide open this turn at bat. But when the first two batters made outs, adding more runs that inning didn't seem likely.

Then the third batter, Fernando Vina, singled to center field. Two pitches later, Placido Polanco made it to first and Vina to second. J. D. Drew came up next. He got a free ride to first base.

Two outs, bases loaded — and Albert Pujols was in the batter's box. The first pitch whistled past him into the catcher's mitt for a called strike. The next was a ball. The third —

Pow! The third connected with the fat part of Pujols's bat and soared into right field, where it dropped to the ground for a double. Vina, Polanco, and Drew all scored, and when Edgar Renteria doubled two batters later, Pujols himself touched home plate for another run.

The Cardinals' lead jumped from 2–1 to 6–1. By the game's end, it had skyrocketed to 10–2. Pujols crossed the plate twice more in the final innings, once after reaching second on a double and once after being walked.

Five days later, Albert posted his first home run of the season in an 8 to 4 win over the Houston Astros. He had added nine more by the end of May as well as chalking up solid numbers in hits, runs, and RBIs. His batting average of .272 wasn't as high as it had been the previous May, but still, it was good enough to keep the media from saying he was in a "sophomore slump" — a term used to describe the weak performance given by many athletes in their second year of professional play.

The media may have been giving Albert a break, but Albert himself was not. He didn't want to be an average player. He didn't want his numbers to stay the same or, worse, go down. He wanted to push himself to be the best player he could be. With that in mind, he worked on his game and tried to learn from his mistakes.

"I learn something new every time I walk into a park," he once said. "Every day, you learn something new, and that's what you want to do to get better and better."

Pujols continued to play the best he could. With help from his bat and his continually improving skills in the field, the Cardinals found themselves in first place by mid-June.

Then tragedy struck. On June 18, the Cardinals' broadcaster, Jack Buck, passed away at age 77. The club and its fans were deeply saddened to lose the man who had voiced their games from 1954 to 2001.

That sorrow turned to shock just four days later. St. Louis was scheduled to play against the Cubs in Chicago. Darryl Kile, a ten-year MLB veteran, was slotted to pitch. Two hours before the game was due to start, however, he was nowhere to be seen.

Concerned, the club contacted the hotel where Kile was staying. Shortly thereafter, they learned

AP/Wide World Photos

Hard hits like this double helped earn Pujols the National League Rookie of the Year in 2001.

AP/Wide World Photos

In a gesture well-known to his fans, Albert Pujols points to the heavens after making a two-run homer in 2003.

AP/Wide World Photos

Even the strongest players need a break now and then—here, Pujols relaxes at first base during a change in pitchers.

AP/Wide World Photos

First baseman Pujols gives it his all and tags out Houston Astro Lance Berkman in a regular season game in 2006.

AP/Wide World Photos

Extra effort is the key to success—as Pujols shows as he begins his slide into home plate during the National League Championship Series in 2006.

AP/Wide World Photos

When it counts, Pujols comes through: a two-run homer in Game 1 of the 2006 World Series.

AP/Wide World Photos

Pujols and teammate Scott Rolen celebrate winning the World Series in 2006!

AP/Wide World Photos

Rain or shine (and here, it's starting to rain), so long as the Cardinals are in the lead, it's all fine with Albert Pujols!

that Kile had been found dead in his room. The cause of death was a narrowing of the arteries that led to the heart.

Anyone who has ever played for a team knows how close teammates become during a season. Kile had been a part of the Cardinals for more than two years. His sudden death left the players stunned and reeling with grief.

Tragedies such as Kile's passing can sometimes cause a team to flounder. But sometimes, they can bring teammates closer together and spur them to fight for victories in the name of the one they've so recently lost.

That's what happened with the Cardinals. Wearing armbands with the initials D.K. and Kile's number, 57, St. Louis held onto first place throughout the second half of the season.

Albert ramped up his play, too, dancing just shy of the .300 mark throughout much of July and August. Then, on August 19, he finally broke through. That game, against the Pittsburgh Pirates, saw him clouting a three-run homer in the third inning that boosted his average from .298 to .301. It dipped down again the next game, but on August 27, he knocked in his 30th home run of the season as well as his 100th RBI to once more top .300.

He never looked back after that. His average rose from .301 to a high of .315 before settling at .314 by the end of the season. In 590 at bats, he had chalked up 34 home runs, 127 RBIs, 118 runs, and 185 hits! Those figures alone were staggering; when taken together with his stats from the previous year, they made him the first player in major-league history to bat better than .300 and hit more than 30 homers, 100 RBIs, and 100 runs in his first two seasons. His combined total of 257 RBIs made him the first player since Ted Williams to beat 250 runs batted in in two seasons.

As the year before, Albert was pleased with his stats. But as before, he knew they meant nothing unless they led to the ultimate goal: the World Series.

Unfortunately, the Cardinals fell short of reaching that goal. After sweeping the Arizona Diamondbacks in the first round, they lost the National League Championship Series to the San Francisco Giants, four games to one.

Pujols was bitterly disappointed, but he tried not to dwell too much on the defeat. He couldn't change the outcome, after all.

But he could do his best to ensure that next year, things would be different.

★ CHAPTER NINE ★

2003

Slugfest!

Boom! Boom! Boom!

Whenever Albert Pujols stepped into the cage for batting practice during the off-season, that sound was sure to be heard. It was a sound he hoped he, his teammates, and their fans would hear hundreds of times in the coming year. To be sure they did, he worked at his swing over . . . and over . . . and over, making adjustments too small for most people to notice.

But Albert knew he was making them, and that's what counted. "You become a good hitter when you can tell yourself what you're doing wrong and correct it the next at bat," he once said.

That Pujols had fixed whatever needed correcting became crystal clear in the first month of the 2003 season.

"Pujols singles . . ."

"Pujols doubles . . ."

"Pujols homers . . ."

His hits, homers, and RBIs kept his name on announcers' lips and in newspaper recaps game after game. At the end of April his batting average was an astonishing .385. On May 2, it reached .390! Then, three weeks later, Pujols turned in one of the most outstanding and well-rounded performances of his career.

The Cardinals were in Pittsburgh to play the first of a three-game series against the Pirates. In his first at bat, Pujols struck out swinging.

Time for one of those minor adjustments, he may have thought. If so, then whatever change he made worked. When he came up to the plate in the fourth inning, he clobbered pitcher Salomon Torres's first throw for an RBI double to left center field.

In the sixth inning, Pujols faced pitcher Joe Beimel. He looked Beimel's first pitch into the catcher's mitt for strike one. Then he watched two more pitches go by for balls one and two. Then came the fourth pitch. *Crack!* Another double to left center.

Fast-forward to the eighth inning, where Pujols faced yet another pitcher, Brian Boehringer. With the count at 2–0, he tapped out a shallow single to right field.

Four at bats, three hits!

Top of the ninth. Another pitcher. Another single!

Five at bats, four hits!

The game went into extra innings. When Pujols came up to bat at the top of the tenth, there were two outs. J. D. Drew stood on third. The Cardinals were up, 9–8, but the Pirates could easily swallow that lead when they came up to bat. But if Pujols could sweeten it by even one run . . .

Pitcher Brian Meadows was hurling for Pittsburgh. He reared back and threw. Ball! Meadows caught the throw back from his catcher. He stared down at Pujols and then went into his windup.

Pujols was best known for his cloud-cutting blasts. But this time, he didn't swing. Instead, he lowered the bat and twisted around to bunt.

Bloop! The ball dribbled toward third. Drew and Pujols took off. Drew reached home safely. It wasn't a run batted in this time; it was a run bunted in!

As stellar as his performance was that game,

Pujols topped it in a fantastic three-day romp in early June. The Cardinals were playing the third of three home games against the Blue Jays. St. Louis had won the first two and was looking forward to sweeping Toronto with a third victory.

Pujols lent a hand — or rather, a bat — early on. In the bottom of the first inning, lead-off batter Miguel Cairo reached first on a single to left field. Jim Edmonds sent him on to third with a ground-rule double. Pujols was up next. He bopped a perfect sacrifice fly into deep right, giving Cairo plenty of time to race home and putting Edmonds in scoring position on third. Unfortunately, Edmonds died on base when the next two batters got out.

Pujols was up again in the third inning. The lead-off batter, he laced the first pitch into right center for a double and later scored on an error.

He came up next in the fourth inning. This time, he singled to center field. He reached second after tagging up following a ground-out by Renteria, but died there when the next batter struck out swinging.

The Blue Jays continued to struggle at the plate each turn at bat. They still hadn't scored by the top of the sixth. The Cardinals, on the other hand, were galloping around the bases and by the bottom of the sixth, had driven the score up to 8–0. Edmonds and Pujols widened that gap even more by blasting back-to-back home runs that inning.

Pujols's homer marked his last trip to the plate that game. Kerry Robinson went in for him at left field in the top of the seventh. That homer also marked Pujols's third hit in three at bats and lifted his batting average to an impressive .379.

Not surprisingly, St. Louis beat Toronto that game with a final score of 13 to 5. The next afternoon, they hosted the Baltimore Orioles for the first of three games. It was an overcast day with temperatures hovering in the mid-sixties — perfect baseball weather.

Albert Pujols started out in left field again. He narrowly missed making an out when Luis Matos clocked a hit into deep left. Matos died on second, however, and the Cardinals came up to bat with the score 0–0.

This game, Pujols was batting third in the order. There were two outs when he approached the plate. He liked the first pitch he saw and laced the ball to center field for a single. Anyone following Pujols's recent outings realized that that single made him

4-for-4 at the plate. While that was a nice stat for Pujols, it didn't add up to a run — and that was all Pujols cared about.

But getting runs that game was proving difficult for both teams. Runners were reaching base but not making it home. Pujols was walked his next at bat — technically considered a hit, bringing his streak to 5 for 5 — but was left hanging as before.

Then, in the bottom of the fourth, the Cardinals broke loose. Three singles were followed by a double by Chris Widger to add up to three runs. Widger reached third on a sacrifice, watched Cairo jog to first after being hit by a pitch, and then ran home on a balked ball to Orlando Palmeiro.

Pujols came to bat with Palmeiro on first and Cairo on second. He watched the first pitch go by for a called strike. He hit the second pitch but the ball flew foul. Then on the third pitch —

Pow! An RBI single to center field! Six times at bat, six hits!

And Albert Pujols wasn't done yet. He had two more trips to the batters' box. The first one came at the bottom of the seventh. The score stood at 5 apiece. Pujols, the lead-off batter, singled to stretch his streak to 7 for 7. He hoped his teammates could send him home to break the tie. Unfortunately, they didn't, and the score remained at 5–5 going into the eighth.

The Orioles gained one their next at bat. The score stuck at Baltimore 6, St. Louis 5 through the first five Cardinal batters in the bottom of the eighth. Then, with J. D. Drew on first, Miguel Cairo on second, and So Taguchi on third, Albert Pujols came up to bat.

Jorge Julio was on the mound for Baltimore. He whipped the first pitch toward the plate.

Pujols swung. *Swish!* Strike one!

Then came Julio's next pitch. This time —

Boom! Pujols swung and connected for a screaming double to left field that scored Taguchi, Cairo, and Drew! The three-run RBI was his eighth hit in eight trips to the plate and gave the Cardinals a two-run lead — which they held to win the game. That blast also jolted Pujols's batting average from .379 to .391!

And was Pujols done yet? He was not! He belted a one-run RBI double in his first at bat against the

Orioles the following afternoon to make his three-game total nine hits for nine at bats.

But as the saying goes, all good things must come to an end. That double was the last of his streak. And that one run was far shy of the eight the Orioles chalked up that day, ending St. Louis's five-game winning streak.

Although Pujols didn't have as many hits in a row as he had had in early June, he did have plenty in the following weeks. On August 16, he reached a milestone by getting a hit in his thirtieth consecutive game. It was the longest such streak in the majors that year, and tied him with Stan Musial for second best in the club's history and left him three games shy of tying the club's number-one streak hitter, Rogers Hornsby, who hit for 33 games in 1922.

"Any time you're [mentioned] with those guys, you're talking about Hall of Famers," Pujols said of how his streak compared with those of Musial and Hornsby. "When you get your name out there with Stan Musial, you're talking about the best hitter who ever played for the Cardinals organization."

Albert's ability at the plate was astonishing, but

what may have been more surprising was how much stronger his play in the field was in 2003. Pujols played first base in 62 games, and left field for 113. Out of 370 innings played at first, he made just one error; in the 904 innings in the field, he made only three. Compared to his stats in the previous two years, those numbers showed a great improvement.

"I've worked my butt off," he admitted of his improved play. "I want to get better in the outfield, and I'm pretty happy where I stand right now. This past season, I got to balls in the outfield that in 2002 and the year before, I couldn't get to."

But for all Pujols's efforts at the plate and in the field, the Cardinals wound up in third place at the end of September. After reaching the playoffs for the last two years, this time they would watch the postseason action from the sidelines.

Pujols was disappointed. But as in the past, he turned his frustration into determination to ensure that the next season, that final outcome would be much different.

But would one player's determination be enough?

★ CHAPTER TEN ★

2004

So Close . . .

Albert Pujols was awarded several baseball honors after the 2003 postseason. On October 22, he was given the Hank Aaron Award as best offensive player in the National League. Two weeks later, he was named the Most Outstanding Player in the National League. That same month, he came in second for the National League's Most Valuable Player, losing out for the second year in a row to Barry Bonds of the San Francisco Giants. He also received his second NL Silver Slugger award.

Pujols no doubt appreciated these acknowledgments of his talent. But what he really wanted — a World Series ring — had so far eluded him. As in years past, he spent the off-season working toward reaching that goal. He lifted weights and made tiny adjustments in the batting cage to perfect his already near-perfect swing. He trained hard at first base, the sole position he was to play in the field in the coming season.

As usual, his training paid off. In the late winter and early spring of 2004, he played in twenty-three exhibition games. When those games were done, he had a batting average of .381 with 10 RBIs. His fielding was crisp and his throws accurate for the majority of plays. There seemed little doubt that he would be a commanding presence in the league again this season.

But to everyone's surprise, Pujols faltered a bit in the early weeks of the regular season. In the Cardinals' opener against the Milwaukee Brewers, he hit an RBI double that tightened the score from 7–4 to 7–6. But he also made a costly fielding error that netted the Brewers two runs — without the Brewers even getting a hit!

Two weeks later, he did something he rarely ever did: in four at bats, he failed to get a single hit. By month's end, he had 25 hits in 87 trips to the plate for an average of .287. When Cardinal fans compared that stat to his average of .385 at the same time the previous year, they couldn't help but worry that Pujols was losing his touch.

They needn't have been concerned. Glimpses of their favorite slugger began to appear in May. In June, he roared back on the scene completely.

On the first day of that month, the Cardinals were playing the Pirates in Pittsburgh. St. Louis was up first. Pujols was third in the batting order. There was one out, a runner at first. Three pitches later, that runner was on third and Albert was on first, thanks to his single to center field. That single started a rally. The inning ended four batters — and three runs — after that.

Albert got up again in the second inning. And again, he got a single. Two ups, two hits, the second an RBI. The Cards led 5–0.

That was the score when Pujols came up again in the top of the fourth. His teammate, Ray Lankford, had just singled off of pitcher Brian Boehringer. Pujols hoped to advance Lankford a base, or maybe two. He did better than that. He hit Lankford home to add two runs to their side!

Three at bats, three hits, two of them RBIs, one of

them a homer. Not a bad day — and it wasn't over yet.

Pujols came back to the plate at the top of the sixth, and clobbered a double to deep center field. And then, unbelievably, *crack!* He slugged *another* double at the top of the ninth to bring his total to five hits in five trips to the plate. It was the second time in his career he had achieved this feat. Interestingly, both times had been in away games against Pittsburgh.

Not that where it happened mattered to Albert Pujols. "I don't think about the park," he said after the game. "Wherever we play, I try to do my best and help our team win."

Win they did that day, by a wide margin of 8–1. They won the next four too, including a game that saw Albert getting four hits in five at bats. Those efforts lofted his average to .325. He looked to be on pace to make it even better until he sprained his left hamstring rounding second base. He took a few games off to let the injury heal. Still his batting average remained near or above .300 for the month of June and the first weeks of July.

The Cardinals, meanwhile, had been absolutely

tearing up the field, winning game after game after game. From July 2 to July 19, they played fourteen matches — and won all but two! With an overall record of 59–34, they were eight games ahead of the second-place Chicago Cubs; on July 20, they added another hash mark to their total wins column.

That game was a showdown between the Cubs and the Cards. Tempers were running high because of incidents that had occurred in the previous game; a few players had nearly come to blows when Cardinal batter Jim Edmonds was hit not once, but twice, by pitches from hurler Carlos Zambrano.

Like that previous game, this one was also punctuated by angry outbursts and physical threats. But it was Albert Pujols's performance that day that captured the headlines.

For the second time in two months, he was 5-for-5 from the plate. Amazingly, three of those hits were homers. The second tied the game at 8–8. The last put the Cards up and over the Cubs for the 11–8 win.

It was the first time in his career he had hit so many home runs in a single game, and of course, Albert was delighted. "It's one of those days you never forget," he told reporters.

Manager Tony La Russa added his own comment, saying, "The best thing about Albert in a very long list of great things is that he plays the game to win."

Win, win, win — that's what the Cardinals kept doing. They were nearly unstoppable. They lost just five games in July to give them a month-end record of 66–39. They lost just five in August, too, out of the 26 games they played, to put them at 87–44.

In the course of that month, Albert racked up more incredible stats. He also hit two career milestones. The first came on August 3, when he slugged a home run in a game against Montreal. It was his thirtieth of the season, making him the first player in MLB history (and the only Cardinal ever) to belt that many in each of his first four years as a professional player.

The second milestone came on August 29 in a game against the Pirates. Albert had taken a rare day off the previous game and came to the match feeling rested and ready. That was good news for the Cardinals.

It was terrible news for the Pirates, however. They had met St. Louis seventeen times so far that season, and lost all but five of those games. Any hope they had of beating the Cardinals began to dim when Pujols came to the plate at the top of the third inning.

Oliver Perez was on the mound for the Pirates. He got two strikes on Pujols before *crack!* Albert laced the third pitch into deep left center for his first triple of the season — and his 100th RBI of the year. That blast earned him a place in MLB history alongside Al Simmons, Ted Williams, and Joe DiMaggio as the only sluggers to drive in 100 or more runs in their first four seasons.

And Pujols wasn't done yet. He led off the top of the eighth inning with a home run to center field! It was the 40th homer for him that season, his second consecutive year of reaching that mark.

"It's aweseome," Albert said of reaching 100 RBIs and 40 home runs in the same game. But he quickly added that he didn't care about the numbers as much as he cared about winning. Helping his team to the postseason and the World Series, that's what was important to him.

That the Cardinals were going to make it to the Championship seemed inevitable. After all, they ended the season with 105 wins and only 57 losses, their club's best record since 1942 as well as the best in the National League Central Division.

But all the season's victories would mean nothing if they couldn't win the first rounds in the postseason. And since they had dropped five of their last seven games, some people wondered if they would even survive the Division Series against the Los Angeles Dodgers.

The first game took place on October 5 in St. Louis. The Dodgers threatened in the first inning with two singles to put men at first and second, only to see those runners die on base.

The Cardinals looked like they might drop out one-two-three after their first two batters got out. Then Albert Pujols came to the plate. He watched one pitch go by for ball one. He watched the second pitch go by, too, but that one was called a strike. Another ball and another strike later, the count was 2-and-2.

On the mound, pitcher Odalis Perez held the ball behind his back and rolled it between his fingertips. He took the signal and then went into his windup.

Whiizzzz! The ball whistled through the air toward the plate.

Pow! Albert sent it sailing through the clear October sky above Busch Stadium. The fans, more than 50,000 of them, jumped to their feet and roared. Home run!

That blast sparked the Cardinals out of their end-of-season slump. They went on to win the game, 8–3. Two nights later, they won again, but then dropped the third game to force a fourth match in the best-of-five series.

The first innings of that fourth game saw both teams scoring two runs apiece. So far, Pujols's bat had been silent, for he had been walked his first time up and then grounded out his second.

His third trip to the plate came at the top of the fourth inning. There were runners at first and second. There were also two outs.

Pitcher Wilson Alvarez threw two balls, a strike, and then another ball to Pujols. With a count at 3–1, other batters might have chosen to watch the next pitch go by. Not Albert. He swung for that fifth pitch with all his might, and when he connected a sound like a pistol shot reverberated around that stadium before being drowned out by the roar of the crowd.

Three-run homer! The Cardinals were up 5–2 —

and when Albert hit an RBI single at the top of the seventh, that three-run lead sweetened to four. That's where the score stayed until the end of the game. St. Louis was the NL Division Series champ!

Albert and his teammates shook hands with all the Dodgers before heading to the locker room to celebrate their victory. They didn't waste too much time congratulating themselves, however; after all, if they were going to make it to the World Series, they had to beat the Houston Astros to become the National League champs first.

They looked on pace to do just that, thanks in very large part to the unbelievable play of their star slugger and first baseman, Albert Pujols. He clobbered a two-run homer in the first inning of the first game and then added another run after reaching base on a walk. In the next game, he was 3-for-4 from the plate, including a game-winning homer at the top of the eighth inning. That belt brought his two-game batting average to .714, or 5 hits in 7 at bats!

Then disaster struck — the Cardinals lost three in a row! One more loss, and it would be Houston, not St. Louis, that went to the World Series.

That loss never came, and again, it was Albert

Pujols who made a big difference. In Game 6, he homered in the first inning, sending Tony Womack across home plate in the bargain to give the Cardinals two runs. He doubled at the bottom of the third and then rounded the last two bases for another run to help St. Louis to a 4–2 lead. That lead tightened to 4–3 at the top of the fourth — and stayed there through the top of the ninth, when Astro Jeff Bagwell clocked a leadoff home run to tie it all up at 4–4!

The score stayed tied through the ninth and into the tenth. It was tied throughout the eleventh, too, forcing the exhausted teams to play a twelfth inning.

Houston didn't score their turn at bat. St. Louis came up, hoping to finally end the match. To do so, they needed just one run.

They got two. The Astros' pitcher walked the first batter, Albert Pujols. Then he got the second to foul out. He got a strike on the third, Jim Edmonds, but then Edmonds connected with the next pitch for a two-run homer!

Was Pujols disappointed that Edmonds was the game's hero instead of him? Hardly! Glory wasn't the name of his game, winning was — and in Game 7, he made sure the Cards won by belting a game-tying RBI double off of pitcher Roger Clemens and then scoring the winning run himself when teammate Scott Rolen homered.

Pujols and the rest of the Cardinals mobbed Rolen, jumping and cheering and laughing with joy. They were going to the World Series for the first time since 1987!

Albert soon had another reason to celebrate. For his performance in the seven-game series, which saw him batting 14-for-28, including 4 home runs and 9 RBIs and an average of .500, Pujols was named the NL Championship Series Most Valuable Player.

"I'm glad to have won the MVP," he told reporters later, "but that trophy is going to stay right in this [locker] room because everybody here is MVP."

Two days after their victory over Houston, the Cardinals headed to Boston to face the Red Sox for the first game of the World Series. Five days after that, they came home — empty-handed. It had taken the Red Sox just four games to do what they hadn't done in eighty-six years: win the World Series.

There would be no celebration, or trophy, in the Cardinal locker room this time.

"It seemed like everything was going their way," Albert Pujols said of the Red Sox. "But we had a great year. I'm proud of the way we battled. . . . We were the second-best team, and nobody expected us to get this far."

Then he added one last thought, something that was familiar to any who knew him: "Now we've got to just prepare ourselves for next year."

✯ CHAPTER ELEVEN ✯

2005

Another Run at the Ring

Albert Pujols had a busy off-season, as usual. He worked on his game. He spent as much time as possible with his family. As a devoted Christian, he also spent time in church and in worship with his family and others who shared his beliefs. He started a new venture as well, one that united the most important pieces of his life into one.

When Albert married Deirdre on New Year's Day in 2000, he became the father to her daughter Isabella. Albert loved that little girl right from the start. He knew that as a child with Down syndrome, she was going to face many challenges in life. He and Deirdre were lucky because they could afford whatever special help, education, and care Isabella might need.

But they knew that not every parent in their

situation was as fortunate. As devout Christians they believed it was their responsibility to help. So in 2005, they launched a charitable organization called the Pujols Family Foundation with the aim of promoting awareness, offering assistance, and providing hope to those living with Down syndrome.

The Foundation was introduced before a game on May 5, 2005, or 5/5/05, in honor of Albert's jersey number. The baseball season was well under way by then, of course, but Albert made it clear that his commitment to the Foundation was every bit as strong as his commitment to the Cardinals. "I want to hit a grand slam off the field," he stated during the press conference held at Busch Stadium.

On the field, he hadn't hit any grand slams so far, but he was batting well. By the time of the press conference, he had racked up 37 hits, 6 of which were home runs and 20 of which were RBIs, in 119 at bats for an average of .339. Five days after the Foundation's launch, he had his best game of the season yet. He came up to bat twice, and hit home runs both times. The second homer scored three runs, and together with the first accounted for all four of the team's runs that day!

Thanks to such performances, the Cardinals were in first place in their division going into the all-star break in July. In fact, their eleven-and-a-half game lead over the second-place Astros was the largest in the St. Louis franchise history. If they kept up that pace, they looked more than capable of returning to postseason again.

That's just what they did, with Albert Pujols leading the charge. By the end of July, he had clobbered 28 home runs and 84 RBIs. People following his career knew that he needed just two more homers to become the first player in major-league history to hit 30 in his first five seasons. And if he hit sixteen more RBIs, he would be the first player in the league to hit 100 for five seasons in a row!

Albert took care of the home run milestone when he slugged number 30 on August 5. As August progressed, he climbed steadily closer to the 100th RBI mark, before finally reaching it on the last day of the month. Typically, he was happier to have won those two games than he was to have gotten his name in the record books.

"I don't think about [breaking records]," he said

after making his 30th home run. "The thing I want is a championship."

The Cardinals edged nearer to a shot at that championship as their regular season drew to a close. Although their record of 100 wins and 62 losses wasn't quite as good as the previous year, it was still the best of any team in the major leagues. St. Louis entered the postseason as the favorites to win the World Series.

Reaching the postseason was due to the whole team's efforts, not the result of any single player's performance. Yet among this talented team, Albert Pujols shone as the brightest star. He ended the regular season with impressive stats, including .330 batting average, 117 RBIs, and 41 home runs.

But of course, those numbers meant nothing unless they added up to a World Series win. And in 2005, that World Series was almost within reach thanks to a showstopping blast from the bat of Albert Pujols in Game 6 of the National League Championship Series.

St. Louis had reached the second round of the playoffs by sweeping the San Diego Padres three games to none in the Division series. Pujols was masterful at the plate in those games, earning 5 hits in 9 at bats for an average of .556.

Unfortunately, their next opponents, the Houston Astros, would prove much more challenging. That was surprising, since in the Cards had beaten the Astros 11 out of 16 times in the regular season. But in this series, Houston seemed to have figured out how to beat St. Louis.

Game 1 went to the Cardinals by a narrow margin of 5 to 3. The hero of that match was St. Louis's Reggie Sanders, whose two-run homer in the first inning made the difference. Pujols helped, too, with an RBI single in the fifth that gave the Cards their fifth run of the day.

But the next day's game was won by the Astros, 4–1, to tie the Series at one game apiece. Then Houston won games 3 and 4 as well, to go up three games to one. They needed just one more victory to step over the Cardinals on their way to the World Series.

They didn't get it their next outing, however. Albert Pujols saw to that, with a hit that may very well go down in the books as the most heroic of his career.

The game was played in Houston. Going into the ninth inning, the Astros led 4–2. Relief pitcher Brad Lidge was on the mound. The first batter he faced was John Rodriguez.

Rodriguez let the first pitch go by for ball one. But he swung on the next three — and missed them all for out number one.

John Mabry came up next. Lidge struck him out, too. Two outs, no one on base. Houston looked to have the game — and the series — in their pocket.

David Eckstein stepped into the batter's box. Lidge worked the count to 1–2. One more strike, and the game would be over.

That strike didn't come. Instead, Eckstein laced the fourth pitch into left field for a single — and then, with Jim Edmonds at bat, reached second base on fielder's indifference. Edmonds was walked, putting runners on first and second.

The Cardinals were still alive, but just barely. They needed a miracle play from the next batter if they were to pull off a win. Luckily, their next batter was Albert Pujols. He swung at Lidge's first pitch — but missed for strike one.

Lidge got the ball back and stared from the

mound to the plate. Pujols stared right back. Lidge reared back and threw. Pujols swung and . . .

Boom! His hit wasn't just strong, it was one of the mightiest blasts ever seen at Houston's Minute Maid Park. The ball flew high beyond the train tracks above the left-field wall for a three-run homer!

Cameras caught the Astros' star pitcher, Andy Pettitte, mouthing the words "oh my," as he watched the ball sail out of sight. Lidge, meanwhile, slowly sank down to a crouch, shaking his head in disbelief.

The Cardinals couldn't believe it, either. "It's the biggest hit I've ever seen," St. Louis pitcher Chris Carpenter said.

Pujols took a moment to follow the ball's flight before beginning his jog around the bases. "I just couldn't believe I did it," he said later.

That blast handed the game to St. Louis and kept them in the running for the National League pennant. The run ended the next night, unfortunately, when the Astros nearly shut the Cardinals out with a 5–1 win to advance to their first World Series in 44 years. Houston fell short there, however, losing to the Chicago White Sox in four straight games.

Pujols hadn't brought home a World Series ring in

2005, but he did have something else to display—his first National League Most Valuable Player trophy. He was the first Cardinal in twenty years to win this award. Characteristically, he gave his team much of the credit for his achievement, saying, "You have to have a great year by your team to win it. You can't do it by yourself."

★ CHAPTER TWELVE ★

2006

Winning It

Albert Pujols entered the 2006 baseball season with a single goal in mind: win the World Series. He began his quest in earnest in April — and proceeded to have one of the most spectacular months of play ever seen.

It started on April 3 with the season opener against the Philadelphia Phillies. Pujols came up to bat in the third inning. *Pow!* He slugged a home run that put the Cardinals ahead 2–0. Two innings later, St. Louis had a very comfortable 10–1 lead when *crack!* Pujols made that lead even more comfortable with a two-run homer. St. Louis won that game easily, 13–5.

Pujols homered in the fifth inning in the next game, too. He added another home run on April 10, bringing his one-week total to four. Five days later, that total increased by one more.

Five home runs in the first two weeks of the season is impressive, but what Pujols did the next two days was nothing short of astonishing.

The Cardinals were playing the last of a three-game series against the Cincinnati Reds. Each team had won a game and were nearly evenly matched with records of 7–4 for the Reds and 6–5 for the Cards. If Albert had anything to do with it, St. Louis was going to leave the third game with a record of 7–5, not 6–6.

He had quite a bit to do with it, as it turned out. The late afternoon game was played in the Cardinals' new and improved Busch Stadium, before a crowd of forty thousand fans. The Reds got on the board first with a run in the first inning. St. Louis answered with two runs of their own in their first at bats, thanks to an RBI triple by John Rodriguez that scored David Eckstein, who had singled, and Pujols, who had been walked. The score stayed 2–1 until the fifth inning — and then Cincinnati opened fire with back-to-back home runs that saw three players crossing the plate.

With the score now 4–2 in favor of the Reds, the Cardinals came up to bat at the bottom of the fifth.

Eckstein started off the inning by flying out to right. Next up was Aaron Miles, who reached first on a single to shortstop and then second on a bad throw to first.

That brought up Albert. He worked the count to 2–2 and then *crack!* connected with the fifth pitch for a home run! He wasn't the only Cardinal flying around the bases that inning, however, for the next batter, Scott Rolen, also blasted a homer to put St. Louis up 5–4.

That one-run lead jumped ahead by one more in the bottom of the seventh inning, when Pujols homered a second time. But the Reds erased their deficit with three runs of their own in the top of the eighth. The Cardinals went through three pitchers that inning in an attempt to stop Cincinnati.

St. Louis could do nothing their turn at bat, but fortunately, the Reds didn't add any more to their side of the board, either. Going into the bottom of the ninth, it was Cincinnati 7, St. Louis 6. A one-run lead is not much, but if the Cardinals didn't get a run or two during their last at bats, it would be enough to give the Reds the win.

Jason Marquis came up first, batting for relief

pitcher Braden Looper. Marquis watched the first pitch into the glove for a strike, and the second for a ball. Then he laced the third into center field for a single.

Albert Pujols came up next. He'd hit home runs his last two at bats, one off pitcher Bronson Arroyo, the other off reliever Rick White. Now he faced a third pitcher, David Weathers. Would Weathers be able to do what his teammates had not—namely, strike Pujols out?

It looked like he would. After his first pitch was called a ball, he caught Pujols looking for a strike.

Pujols swung at the third pitch. *Crack!* A hit! But no, the ball went foul. Strike two.

Weathers went into his windup and hurled the fourth pitch.

Boom! That sound was well known to many people in the park. It was the sound of Albert Pujols slugging a home run! But this wasn't just any home run: it was his third straight of the night, a 441-foot blast that was good for two runs and a victory for the Cardinals!

Pujols was grinning broadly when he rounded the bases. He was so happy that, just before he reached home plate, he did a little jig! "Hey, you get a walk-off home run, you get to do whatever you want," he joked.

It was his eighth home run of the month, and he wasn't done yet. In his first at bat of the next game, against the Pittsburgh Pirates, he homered yet again to make it four in a row. He was only the second player in major-league history to accomplish such a feat. And was he done yet?

He was not. Nine home runs so far that month turned into ten, and then eleven, twelve, thirteen, and finally, on April 29, he hit his fourteenth to give the Cardinals the win in a hard-fought game against the Washington Nationals.

Fourteen home runs in less than a month? Unbelievable — and one better than the previous record set by Ken Griffey, Jr., in 1997.

By this time, the sports media was going insane over Albert Pujols. He added fuel to their fire by hitting 11 additional home runs in May, causing many to predict that he would slug more than 80 by the season's end. He also led the league in RBIs, a fact which had helped his team to their 34–19 record at the end of May.

Then something unexpected happened. While stretching high to catch a foul ball near first base in a game, Albert pulled his right oblique, a big muscle in his side. The pain was so severe that he stopped short in mid-play.

The diagnosis was grim, for there was no quick cure for such a bad muscle strain. Pujols was expected to be sidelined for as long as six weeks. Fortunately, he ended up only sitting on the bench for half that long and the Cardinals managed to hold onto their lead in the National League Central Division without him.

Albert returned to the lineup on June 22. That game, he got up to bat 4 times but failed to get a hit. A day later, however, he roared back to life with 4 hits in 4 at bats, one of them a homer! He also showed that he was fully recovered from his oblique injury when he leaped for a catch at first base.

Because of his time spent on the disabled list, his home run count was lower than predicted by the all-star break. Still, by mid-July he had once again surpassed the 30 home run mark. His 30th came in spectacular fashion, a game-winning blast that won a long 14-inning match against the Los Angeles

Dodgers on July 16. It was the second time that month he ended an extra-inning match with a walk-off home run. The 14th-inning home run made it six consecutive seasons that he had hit 30 — and considering he'd sat out for three weeks of games, the accomplishment was all the more remarkable.

But Albert didn't care. He hit home runs — and singles, doubles, triples, and RBIs — to win games, not break records. The Cardinals were winning games, although not as many as they had in past years. By the end of July, their record stood at 58–46; their record at the same time the previous years had been 66–38. Still, those 58 wins were more than any other team had earned in the NL Central division. If they could stay on top for the remainder of the season, they'd make it into the playoffs for the third year in a row.

Albert did all he could to make sure they stayed on top, but sometimes, even his best efforts weren't enough to give them the win. On August 22, for example, he belted in a three-run homer in the fourth to put the Cardinals up 3–1 over the New York Mets. Then on his very next trip to the plate he hit another home run, this one a grand slam that gave

St. Louis a commanding 7–1 lead and Pujols a career high of 7 RBIs.

And yet, somehow, the Cardinals lost the game, 8–7.

Pujols worked hard to help his teammates put such disappointments behind them and to stay focused on the ultimate goal: a trip to the World Series. With such a player leading the charge, they drew closer to that goal with every passing day.

When the regular season ended, the Cardinals were still in first place in their division, although just barely. Their record of 83–78 was their worst in years; their win-loss tally of 12 and 17 from September 1 to October 1 had many observers predicting that they would be bounced from the playoffs in the first round.

No one seemed to have mentioned that to the Cardinals, however. They faced the San Diego Padres for the Division title. Four games and three wins later, they left the Padres in the dust to move on to the NL Championships.

Here, they traded wins and losses with the powerful New York Mets to reach a 3–3 tie and force the series into a final, seventh game. Albert had had some good moments in the duel so far, including a fifth-game home run that gave the Cardinals a win, but this last game, the glory belonged to his teammate, Yadier Molina. With the game tied at one apiece at the top of the ninth, Molina clobbered a two-run homer. When the Mets couldn't answer with runs of their own, the Cardinals were on their way to the World Series for the second time in three years!

Their opponents for the World Championship title were the Detroit Tigers, a team that had wallowed in or near the cellar for several years before turning things around in 2006. They amazed everyone by besting the New York Yankees to take the Division title, and then sweeping the Oakland Athletics to advance to their first World Series in 22 years.

The Tigers had played eight games on their way to the World Series, the last on October 14. They had a full week to recover before the start of the championships on Saturday, October 21. The Cardinals, on the other hand, had played eleven games, including the last one on October 19, just two days prior to the first match of the Series. Many wondered how

St. Louis would fare against the much more rested Detroit team.

They found out soon enough.

The Tigers drew first blood when the Cardinals' rookie pitcher, Anthony Reyes, gave up a double, a walk, and then a single for a run.

But St. Louis stormed back, with a home run by Scott Rolen in the top of the second followed by three more runs in the third. There were two outs when Molina scored the first of those three on an RBI double that left Chris Duncan on second — and saw Albert Pujols striding to the plate.

It was then that the Tigers made a big mistake. When there are two outs, a runner on second, and a powerful hitter coming up to bat, the best thing to do is walk that batter. Instead, Detroit decided to pitch to Pujols.

Pujols took full advantage of their error in judgment. When the 93-mile-an-hour fastball reached him, he didn't just hit it — he sent it sailing far over the right-field fence for a two-run homer!

The Tigers pitched more carefully to Pujols after that. But even when he wasn't hitting, he was a threat. After he was walked early in the sixth inning, he reached third base on a throwing error, and then raced home to score the team's seventh run.

Albert didn't get up again that game, but it didn't matter. The supposedly exhausted Cardinals took the game, 7–2, from the well-rested Tigers.

The next night, however, it was a different story. The Tigers clawed their way to an early two-run lead and kept the Cardinals, including Pujols, hitless until the very end. The game went to Detroit, 3–1.

The Series moved from Detroit to St. Louis for Game 3. It was a chilly afternoon, but that didn't stop the hometown fans from crowding into the stands to cheer on their team. And they had every reason to cheer. Not only did the Cardinals win the game by posting five runs, they kept the Tigers from crossing home plate even once!

St. Louis scored five runs the next game, too, but this time the Tigers almost beat them. Almost, but not quite. The Cardinals won, 5–4, to go up in the series 3–1. And then, the next night, they won again, 4–2, to become the new champions of baseball!

That final game wasn't an easy battle, or a particularly pretty one for the Tigers, who committed costly errors, one of which resulted in a run for the

Cardinals. Pujols made the most interesting play of the night, a lunging catch off the bag followed by a throw from flat on his back to his teammate at first for the out.

But overall, that game — in fact, the whole World Series — had not featured the outstanding plays, crackerjack hits, and exciting moments that fans looked for from the two best teams in the league. Instead, the Series had been marked by sluggish batting, unforced errors, and downright silly controversies such as the question of whether a smudge on a pitcher's hand was just dirt or some illegal substance used to make his pitches move oddly.

Pujols himself had not had the kind of postseason many believed he could produce. In the course of five games, he went to the plate 15 times, but had only 3 hits, 1 home run, and 2 RBIs. His batting average was a dismal .200.

No doubt Pujols was disappointed not to have been more of a help to his team. But if nothing else, the fact that the Cardinals had won the World Series without a stronger performance from their star slugger proved one thing: winning games was a team effort, not the work of one player.

"We were the underdogs," Pujols reminded everyone later. "We turned it around when we needed to. We believed in ourselves and we came through."

Believing had finally helped Albert Pujols earn the World Series ring he had dreamed of for so long. He also received another honor, his first Golden Glove award, given to him for his outstanding play at first base. And while he didn't win the National League MVP award that year, he still had some of the best offensive stats in the league, including a career high of 49 home runs, the second greatest number of RBIs in the league (137), and the third-best batting average (.331).

✯ CHAPTER THIRTEEN ✯

2007 and Beyond

Believing

Albert Pujols took a little time to rest after the 2006 World Series, before tackling some new ventures off the field. In January of 2007, he traveled to the Dominican Republic to take part in an international relief effort aimed at helping poor children of that nation. "This is a trip that we've been planning for almost a year," he said shortly before departure. "I'm taking six doctors and two assistants down to the Dominican. As of right now, we have three villages that we're going to work on, and we've got 1,000 kids that we're going to work with in six days."

After he returned home from that journey, he studied up for an important exam. On February 7, he took and aced the test to become an official citizen of the United States.

Soon afterward, he reported to Florida for the

Cardinals' spring training camp. He was a week early and spent the time working out. He knew that if he and his teammates were to defend their championship title, they needed to be in tip-top condition and to play together like a well-oiled machine. He wanted to be sure he did his part.

Unfortunately, the 2007 Cardinals simply weren't as strong or as scrappy as the 2006 Cardinals had been. After a decent showing in the preseason, they lost four of their first five games of the schedule, including a devastating 10–0 loss to the New York Mets.

Just as troubling as these losses was the silence coming from the bat of Albert Pujols. In those five games, he had come to the plate 17 times — and gotten just a single hit! Fans wondered if their favorite slugger was headed for a season-long slump, or if he would recover his swing.

They got their answer the next game. St. Louis was playing Houston and had a one-run lead going into the top of the third inning. There was one out and a runner at first when Albert Pujols came up to bat. He let the first pitch go by for a called strike. The next pitch was a ball. The third — *pow!* The third took off like a rocket launched from Pujols's bat! It was his first homer of the season, and his first RBI.

He had a decent game the Cardinals' next outing, too, adding two hits in three at bats. But then his bat grew quiet again. By the end of April, Pujols had only 23 hits, 15 RBIs, and 6 home runs. His average had hovered closer to .250 than the .300 it usually reached.

St. Louis was posting lower-than-usual numbers too, winning just 10 out of 24 games, their worst April showing in years. They didn't improve much in May — or, to their great disappointment, in June. In fact, by the all-star break in July, the Cardinals were only 40 and 45, just good enough for third place in the NL Central Division.

And how was Albert Pujols faring? His offensive stats had improved, earning him a .300 or higher batting average for most of the weeks leading up to the break. He had 96 hits and 52 RBIs, but only 16 homers. Unless he started connecting more powerfully in the weeks after the July hiatus, it seemed he wouldn't reach the 30-home-run mark this year.

But hitting for more power, and distance, and home runs, was just what Albert did after the break.

By the end of July, his home run total was up to 23. In August, he went on a home run tear, blasting five in five consecutive games between August 17 and August 22. The last of those five marked his 30th of the season — and made Albert Pujols one of the only players in major-league history to post 30 or more homers in his first seven seasons.

Was he pleased to have chalked up another personal record? Probably, but as always, what he achieved personally was nothing if it didn't win games.

"I don't play for numbers. I play to accomplish some goals," he said in late August. "And my goal is to win as many World Series as I can and to be in as many playoffs as I can."

But by the beginning of September, it was clear to everyone that the Cardinals would not reach the playoffs, let alone the World Series, that year. That month saw them losing nine in a row, their worst losing streak in years. It also saw Albert Pujols sitting on the bench resting a strained left calf muscle.

Rest, however, was not something Albert took to easily, especially when his team's record was on the line. When he got back into the lineup, he was raring to go. With that kind of momentum, it wasn't surprising that he set yet another MLB record. On September 26, he clocked his 32nd home run of the season, a home run that was also his 100th RBI of 2007.

Those RBIs and homers put him in the history books as the only player in major-league history to reach the 100 and 30 milestones in the first seven seasons of his career. Not even Hall-of-Fame slugger Ted Williams, who had hit 100 RBIs in his first seven seasons, had hit 30 or more home runs in those same years.

"Since his rookie year he's had us scratching our heads in amazement at the quality of his baseball," Cardinals manager Tony La Russa said of Pujols's achievement.

Sadly, nothing Pujols or anyone else on the Cardinals achieved in September could turn the team around. The reigning world champs had languished in third place throughout the season, and when they played their final game on September 30, that's where they ended.

For his part, Pujols concluded with a satisfactory batting average of .327, plus 185 hits, 32 homers,

103 RBIs, and 99 runs — the first season he failed to surpass the 100 mark in that category. He would have traded in all the best stats in the world, however, if only his team had made it into the playoffs. Instead, he and his fellow Cardinals watched from the sidelines as the Boston Red Sox tore through the postseason to win their second World Series in four years.

☆ EPILOGUE ☆

He Didn't

Less than two months after the 2007 World Series, the Mitchell Report was published. People the world over tuned in to see which baseball players were named in the investigation into performance-enhancing drug use in Major League Baseball.

Albert Pujols tuned in, too — and to his complete shock, he learned that a local television station had been insisting his name was among those listed in the investigation.

It turned out that the station was wrong. A source in New York had leaked faulty information about the Mitchell Report before the report was official. Rather than verify the information or wait for the actual report to be made public, the television crew chose to report the leaked list as fact. When the real

Report came out at two o'clock, Albert's name was nowhere in it.

Albert was furious to have had his name besmirched, but dealt with the situation in an appropriate manner by issuing a statement through his agent.

"I have never disrespected, nor cheated the game of baseball and knew without a doubt that my name would not be mentioned in the official investigation. . . . What concerns me is the effect this has had on my family and that my character and values have now been questioned due to the media's lack of accuracy in their reporting. . . . I would like to thank my fans for their continued support and never doubting my integrity. God has blessed me and allowed me to play a game that I would never take for granted."

In later interviews, he still seemed flabbergasted at having been accused of taking or injecting drugs to help his game.

"Since 2001, I've been proving myself every year," he said. "How much better can I get? Only God knows. Do I need to cheat in this game to get better?

This is a hobby, man. I fear God too much to do stupid things in this game. Cheating on this game, that's not right."

Pujols was never part of the substance abuse scandal that is still tarnishing the reputations of so many players in the major leagues. He is one of the good guys, a player who has reached the heights of the game by perfecting the talent he was born with through hard work and dedication. Off the field, he is just as dedicated to his church, his family, and his many charitable causes.

Albert Pujols is now in his eighth year as a professional, and while he has been slowed at times by injuries and has experienced slumps like any other player, he has always bounced back. The twenty-eight-year-old has broken several records and will probably set others in the seasons ahead. He has his first World Series ring, and hopes to help his team earn more.

But even if a second ring never happens, Pujols won't despair. His family will be there to support him and his faith will carry him through any tough times to come. He will always be able to look back on his accomplishments with pride and the knowledge that he earned them honestly.

"God has blessed me," Albert says on his Family Foundation Web site — and if it is so, then the baseball world must be forever thankful.

Albert Pujols's Year-to-Year Batting Statistics

SEASON	TEAM	G	AB	R	H	2B	3B	HR	RBI	BB	SO	SB	CS	AVG	OBP	SLG	OPS
2001	StL	161	590	112	194	47	4	37	130	69	93	1	3	.329	.403	.610	1.013
2002	StL	157	590	118	185	40	2	34	127	72	69	2	4	.314	.394	.561	.955
2003	StL	157	591	137	212	51	1	43	124	79	65	5	1	.359	.439	.667	1.106
2004	StL	154	592	133	196	51	2	46	123	84	52	5	5	.331	.415	.657	1.072
2005	StL	161	591	129	195	38	2	41	117	97	65	16	2	.330	.430	.609	1.039
2006	StL	143	535	119	177	33	1	49	137	92	50	7	2	.331	.431	.671	1.102
2007	StL	158	565	99	185	38	1	32	103	99	58	2	6	.327	.429	.568	.997
Total	—	1091	4054	847	1344	298	13	282	861	592	452	38	23	.332	.420	.620	1.040

Albert Pujols's Year-to-Year Career Highlights

2001:

- National League Rookie of the Year
- National League Sliver Slugger
- Reached NL Division Series

2002:

- Finished second in National League Most Valuable Player voting
- Reached NL Championship Series

2003:

- National League Silver Slugger
- Finished second in National League Most Valuable Player voting
- Hank Aaron Award

2004:

- National League Silver Slugger
- Finished third in National League Most Valuable Player voting
- Reached World Series

2005:

- National League Most Valuable Player
- Reached NL Championship Series

2006:

- National League Gold Glove (first base)
- Member of the World Series Champions

MATT CHRISTOPHER®

THE #1 SPORTS SERIES FOR KIDS

Read them all!

- Baseball Flyhawk
- Baseball Turnaround
- The Basket Counts
- Body Check
- Catch That Pass!
- Catcher with a Glass Arm
- Catching Waves
- Center Court Sting
- Centerfield Ballhawk
- Challenge at Second Base
- The Comeback Challenge
- Comeback of the Home Run Kid
- Cool as Ice
- The Diamond Champs
- Dirt Bike Racer
- Dirt Bike Runaway
- Dive Right In
- Double Play at Short
- Face-Off
- Fairway Phenom
- Football Double Threat
- Football Fugitive
- Football Nightmare
- The Fox Steals Home
- Goalkeeper in Charge
- The Great Quarterback Switch
- Halfback Attack*
- The Hockey Machine
- Hot Shot
- Ice Magic
- Johnny Long Legs
- Karate Kick

*Previously published as Crackerjack Halfback

The Kid Who Only Hit Homers
Lacrosse Face-Off
Lacrosse Firestorm
Line Drive to Short**
Long-Arm Quarterback
Long Shot for Paul
Look Who's Playing First Base
Miracle at the Plate
Mountain Bike Mania
Nothin' But Net
Penalty Shot
Power Pitcher***
The Reluctant Pitcher
Return of the Home Run Kid
Run For It
Shoot for the Hoop
Shortstop from Tokyo
Skateboard Renegade
Skateboard Tough
Slam Dunk
Snowboard Champ
Snowboard Maverick
Snowboard Showdown
Soccer Duel
Soccer Halfback
Soccer Hero
Soccer Scoop
Stealing Home
The Submarine Pitch
The Team That Couldn't Lose
Tennis Ace
Tight End
Top Wing
Touchdown for Tommy
Tough to Tackle
Wingman on Ice
The Year Mom Won the Pennant

All available in paperback from Little, Brown and Company

**Previously published as Pressure Play

***Previously published as Baseball Pals

Matt Christopher®

Sports Bio Bookshelf

Muhammad Ali

Lance Armstrong

Kobe Bryant

Jennifer Capriati

Dale Earnhardt Sr.

Jeff Gordon

Ken Griffey Jr.

Mia Hamm

Tony Hawk

Ichiro

LeBron James

Derek Jeter

Randy Johnson

Michael Jordan

Peyton and Eli Manning

Yao Ming

Shaquille O'Neal

Albert Pujols

Jackie Robinson

Alex Rodriguez

Babe Ruth

Curt Schilling

Sammy Sosa

Tiger Woods